of a

Immanent nature of samsara and nirvana
the clear light
the saintly Dharma shows the mode of being
the clear light
may the fortunate ones who practice
the mahamudra-clear light
become Buddhas in the heart of Awakening
the clear light

BOKAR RINPOCHE

The Day
of a Buddhist Practitioner

Bokar Rinpoche

English translation Christiane Buchet

ClearPoint Press
San Francisco, California

The Day of a Buddhist Practitioner

Published by:
ClearPoint Press
PO Box 170658
San Francisco, CA 94117

The original text of this book was published in French and was titled **La journée du pratiquant.**
Copyright reserved for all countries:
Association Claire Lumière, Mas Vinsargues, 13116 Vernègues, France.

Copyright © 1998 English Edition
ClearPoint Press
Printed in the United States of America
Printed on acid-free paper
Library of Congress Catalog Card Number: 98-70366

PUBLISHER'S ACKNOWLEDGEMENT

The Publisher gratefully acknowledges the generous help of Jason Espada, Rosemary Gilpin, Karen Graham, Michael DeNoya, Derek Smith, Elson Snow, Carolyn Sumrall, Isao and Sets Tanaka.

Cover Ink Drawing by Carolyn Sumrall

Introduction

Sutra 佛學,經典

Karma 業

FOUR FACTORS OF AWAKENING

Awakening is true happiness, temporally and ultimately. It is the essence of all the qualities, but Awakening can be attained only if four factors are present: the primary cause, the support, the helping condition, and the means.
— The primary cause is the potential state of Awakening, naturally and universally present in the minds of all beings.
— The support is a human existence, higher than any other existence from a spiritual point of view. If put into practice to attain Awakening, it is called a precious human existence.
— The helping condition is a qualified spiritual teacher, one who shows us the unmistaken way.
— The means are instructions given by the teacher in the framework of various teachings left by the Buddha, whether sutras or tantras.[1]

Without these four factors, we cannot progress toward Awakening. Absence of even one factor makes the others inoperative. All four are now gathered for us. It is up to us to use them in a beneficial way in this life.

Chakra 輪, 脈輪

Nirvana 涅槃

Dakas 勇父 (男)

Dakinis 空行 (女)

Let us think of our present good fortune and of the positive activity of our past lives that made it possible. Let us rejoice and progress on the path.

A LIFE TOWARD AWAKENING

Giving up the ordinary activities of this world and devoting ourselves only to spiritual practice create the ideal conditions for inner progress. In this perspective, it is necessary to learn Tibetan language because the Buddhist teachings in their totality are kept presently in this language, and translations into Western languages are still rare. We can then complete a three-year retreat and continue our practice by additional retreat of months or years. Devoting our entire life to study, reflection, and spiritual practice is the best use we can make of our lives.

If it is not possible to devote ourselves entirely to the Dharma in a full and exclusive way, we can, however, implant the Dharma in our daily lives through simple and regular practices, such as Chenrezig meditation, and we can vacation in a Dharma center to deepen our knowledge near a lama, meditate with other people, and even do short retreats of one to several weeks.

Even if the latter possibilities are closed to us and we have no opportunity to stay at a Dharma center, we can still practice during our daily life and benefit from this.

If we devote even a very small amount of time to practicing the Dharma on a regular and daily basis, this small amount will accumulate day after day, and after months or years, the results will be far from negligible. We will form the habit of a spiritual life and accumulate a great deal of positive potential. We will rid ourselves of many negative habits and avoid many negative deeds.

The positive and negative coloration of our deeds comes from habits imprinted in our mind. Deeds that we accomplish under the influence of these positive or negative habits will produce karmic results and will ripen. Engendering even a single positive thought imprints a positive habit in our mind. Activities of speech and body leave an imprint in our mind in the same way.

Every day, we must be careful with our physical, verbal, and mental behavior in order to eliminate any negative aspect, and develop the most positive attitude possible. This will transform us.

真性

As long as we have not realized that the mode of being of our mind[2] resides in the union of relative truth and absolute truth—a realization that corresponds to Awakening—these two truths[3] are conceived as separate instead of being seen in their unity.

Positive and negative deeds are lacking reality from an ultimate point of view, although from the relative point of view their consequences are inescapable. Positive activity necessarily results in happiness for the doer of the deed; negative activity necessarily results in suffering. This play of relationships characterizes relative truth. Until we realize ultimate reality, we are subject to the inescapable functioning of relative reality, although this reality is lacking reality in itself. That is why it is essential to know how to discriminate positive from negative, to recognize what must be practiced and what must be given up.[4]

It is true that the accomplishment of positive or negative activity depends solely on the mind. Imprints of deeds are fixed only in the mind, and the mind alone experiences the result of deeds in the form of happiness or suffering. Although the mind alone is concerned with accomplishing deeds, storing them, and experiencing their consequences, this process is also an infallible process in the framework of relative truth.

Even if fire does not exist from an ultimate point of view, if we place our hand in the fire, we immediately burn ourselves.

Until we have realized this ultimate reality, let us adopt a positive type of activity and reject the negative.

MENTAL IMPRINTS

In the domain of relative truth, deeds leave mental imprints on our mind. The process of memory gives us a simple illustration of what they are. We can think now, "I must do some errands at five o'clock." This thought then leaves the surface of our mind. However, it remains as an imprint. That is why, when the time comes, it reappears and we can say, "It is time to do the errands." Such are the imprints: images of a current that are later re-actualized.

Imprints are characterized by becoming more rigid and constraining as the deeds that create them are repeated. Alcohol is an obvious example. The first time a person drinks alcohol, no pleasure is felt but a bitter, burning sensation is experienced. If the person continues to drink a little each day, the unpleasant impression is eliminated and replaced by pleasure. Finally, the person likes the taste of alcohol. Soon the moment arrives when the habit is so strongly rooted that the person cannot do without alcohol. What happened? A deeper and deeper imprint formed in the mind and became an addictive characteristic.

The same process occurs when we form positive imprints for a spiritual life. Initially, it is often difficult to form positive habits; however, gradually, what we do by first imposing an effort on ourselves becomes easier, and we end up discovering great joy in it. Our mind and the Dharma blend together. When we meditate, it is the Dharma; when we do not meditate it is also the Dharma. Acquiring these positive imprints is very important and cannot be achieved without continuity. Practicing one day and neglecting practice the next day is not sufficient. For the positive habit to become stronger, regularity and perseverance are necessary. After some months or years, we become aware that our negative tendencies have decreased, and our positive tendencies have bloomed. We must stay on the path until Awakening.

Imprints left by negative deeds are not irremediable. It is possible to undo them by regretting and disapproving of them. Imprints are then neutralized and their karmic result will not occur. On the contrary, without regretting and disapproving them, negative imprints, if left to themselves, increase each day. A small negative deed accomplished today, if we do not disapprove of it, creates an imprint that deepens each day in our mind. It is a little like money that, deposited in the bank, produces interest each day. But, in the case of negative deeds, the interest works against us until we redeem it in the form of great suffering.

If we do not pay attention, positive imprints can also be nullified. An angry move or other negative feeling can destroy all the merit of a positive deed if we have not dedicated it earlier to the benefit of all beings. Dedication not only preserves acquired merit but allows it to grow day after day.[5]

FROM RELATIVE TO ULTIMATE TRUTH

As long as we are not beyond relative truth, causal relationships between positive/negative deeds and happiness/suffering will continue to rule our existence. We are only beginners and cannot immediately realize ultimate truth. Our practice, above all, is on the level of the relative. When we adopt the correct attitude in the framework of this relative truth and reject all its negative aspects, our mind gains a quality that gradually leads to realization of ultimate truth. Skillful use of the relative progressively opens the ultimate to us.

Beginners can have only a limited approach to ultimate truth through meditation. They must devote themselves mainly to working within the framework of the relative. Then, their inner development gradually leads them to a stage where both aspects find a balance in the practice: on one side, meditation and understanding of ultimate truth; on the other side, activity in the relative domain through working of body, speech, and mind. The deeper the realization of ultimate truth becomes, the less important the practices requiring an effort of the body, speech, and mind are.

For us beginners, only meditating on the ultimate mode of being is extremely difficult. This must be supported by the active participation of our physical, verbal, and mental activity, by an effort to reject the negative and adopt the positive. Therefore, steady daily practice is necessary.

A Certain Change

Those who follow the Buddha's teachings must experience a certain change in their conduct, in the way they express themselves, and in their way of thinking. Without this change, even though entering the gate of the teachings marks our mind with a happy imprint, we do not obtain great results.

We might soak black fabric in red, yellow, blue, or green dye; it will never become red, yellow, blue, or green. We might leave it for hours or for days; no modification will occur. In a similar way, if no change occurs within us, it is the sign of absence or insufficiency of our practice.

On the contrary, when we soak white fabric in a dye, it takes the color. For instance, when soaked in yellow, at best, it will become bright yellow. But, if the fabric does not take the color well, it will not stay completely white, it will become a dull yellow. It is the same with our spiritual practice; if done perfectly, at best we will attain Awakening in this lifetime. However, if we do not attain the ideal result, at least a certain change must occur. Our activity and speech at least must become slightly more positive than before having taken Refuge. Our mind must at least be less occupied by ill will or covetousness but be occupied by good will, contentment, compassion, and faith.

We must be like white fabric that can be dyed and not like black fabric that never changes. To do that, daily practice is indispensable.

Green Tara

綠度母

Milestones for the Day

1- The First Thought of the Day
In order to do morning practices, we must make the effort to get up 15 minutes earlier than usual.[6]

Waking up, we sit on the bed in meditation posture, we relax, and we think:

May all beings get up from the bed of samsara.[7]

Samsara and suffering are like a bed; karma, passions, and illusions are like sleeping. When we wake up and sit on the bed, we, therefore, wish that all beings rid themselves of karma, passions, and ignorance, and that they wake up to knowledge.

Then we think:

May they attain the Absolute Body of Awakening.

Buddha nature—Awakening in a causal state—is present in the mind of all beings. We wish for this potential to shed the sleep of illusion and the karma that covers it, and that all beings swiftly attain the Absolute Body, manifested Awakening.

19

As far as possible, we express these wishes aloud; otherwise we can recite them mentally.

2- Breathing Exercises
a) Expulsion of Residual Breath
Sitting on the bed, we inhale deeply. When we exhale, we stretch out our fingers while our hands rest on our knees. Exhaling must be light in the beginning, stronger in the middle, and light again at the end. Although we exhale through the nose, at the same time, we think that we reject the air through the mouth and all the pores of our skin. We imagine that the exhaled air is black in color; that it carries bad karma, veils, and conflicting emotions accumulated since time without beginning; and that all these negative aspects are disappearing into the distance. We then deeply inhale while closing the hands. We think that the compassion and blessing of the Buddhas and Bodhisattvas, taking the shape of a light of five colors (white, blue, yellow, red, and green) enter through the nose, mouth, and pores, and circulate throughout our body.

We do three cycles of inhaling/exhaling.

b) Union of Breath and Mind
After having exhaled the residual breath, we breathe naturally. Relaxed, and without distraction,

20

we focus our entire attention on breathing, mind and breathing having become one.

We do this for seven breathing cycles.

c) Sacred Breathing of the Vajrayana 金剛乘
If we have received empowerments, we associate breathing with the three syllables OM AH HUNG that include the essence of all mantras and represent the Body, Speech, and Mind of all the Buddhas. Consequently, they also contain the essence of all empowerments we have received.

When we inhale, we imagine that a white light enters into us while at the same time we mentally say the syllable OM. Having arrived at the maximum of the inhalation, we imagine that our heart and chest are filled with a red light and at the same time we mentally say the syllable AH. Finally, while exhaling, we imagine that the breath that we expel out of our body takes the shape of a blue light and at the same time we mentally say the syllable HUNG.

We do this three times.

3- Orienting Our Mind
Before leaving the bed, we give the right orientation to our mind for the day to come. We commit ourselves to practice as much as possible by thinking:

21

Today, from this instant on to the moment in the evening when I fall asleep, I will exert myself to accomplish all the positive and reject all the negative. I will practice the spiritual path to become able to help all beings be free from suffering and progress toward liberation.[8]

We do not think so much that our practice is benefiting ourselves alone, but rather that through it, we will develop qualities that will allow us to rid others of suffering and lead them to the definitive and genuine happiness that is Awakening.

It is important to give our mind this momentum for the day and strengthen it by resolving that we will not forget the commitments taken in the morning.

We think:

Today, I will avoid causing harm through my physical activity
I will avoid causing harm through my speech
I will avoid causing harm through my thoughts
Today, I will do my best to engage in beneficial physical activity
I will do my best to speak useful and pleasant words
I will do my best to nourish well wishing thoughts for all beings

Then we get up and wash ourselves.

Dorje Sempa, Purification Buddha

金剛薩陲

4- Washing That Purifies

If we have received the Dorje Sempa empowerment or know this practice, while washing ourselves, we meditate in the following way.

Dorje Sempa is in the space in front of us. From his body, a luminous nectar flows and washes our body inwardly and outwardly. We think that we are purified from the negative karma and veils staining our body, speech, and mind. We can supplement this practice by reciting the short or long Dorje Sempa mantra.

When we finish washing, we think that Dorje Sempa melts into us.

If we do not know the meditation of Dorje Sempa, we simply think of soap and water ridding us from negative karma and veils covering our mind. However, we can add to this thought the recitation of the Dorje Sempa mantra if we know it.

5- Making Offerings

It is important, if possible, to arrange a small shrine in our home. On a shelf or piece of furniture, we place a statue or a picture of the Buddha, in front of whom we place the seven traditional offerings: drinking water, washing water, flowers, incense, light, perfumed water, food, and music.[9]

Having purified ourselves by washing, we make offerings.

Facing the shrine, we then prostrate three times reciting the mantra.

KUNCHO SUM LA CHASELLO
OM NAMO MENJU SHIRIYE
NAMO SU SHIRIYE
NAMO UTAMA SHIRIYE SOHA

While prostrating, we imagine that facing us in space are the Three Jewels and the Three Roots.[10] We mentally place ourselves under their protection. The mantra increases the benefit of prostrating.

6- Homage to the Buddha

We sit in front of the shrine or facing a statue or picture of the Buddha. If we do not have a picture or statue, we imagine ourselves in front of the Buddha as he is usually represented, wearing a yellow monk robe and holding a begging bowl.

We think that the Buddha gathers in his essence all the aspects of Refuge and we pray to him, reciting three times:

LAMA TONPA CHOMDENDE DESHINSHEKPA DRACHOMPA YANGDAKPAR ZOPO SANGYE PAL GYALWA SHAKKYATUPPA LA CHATSELLO, CHO SU KHYAB SUCHIO, JIN GY LAB TU SOL.

Pure and perfect Buddha, glorious and victorious Sakyamuni, you are the master, teacher, the Lord, Thus-Gone, and Victor over all enemies. I pay homage to you and place myself under the protection of your teaching. Grant me your blessing.[11]

We then recite the Sakyamuni mantra seven or twenty times:

TAYATA OM MUNI MUNI MAHA MUNAYE SOHA

7- Taking Refuge 皈依

Still sitting in front of the shrine, we recite the prayer of taking Refuge. If we know the whole representation of all aspects of Refuge as described in the preliminary practices, we imagine that we are in front of them. Otherwise, we simply visualize Sakyamuni Buddha facing us in space, or our root lama or our yidam (Chenrezig or another one) with the thought that they gather in themselves all the aspects of Refuge.

We recite one of the three Refuge prayers[12] seven times:

Long form

PALDEN LAMA DAMPA NAMLA KHYAB SU CHIO

YIDAM KHILKHOR GI LHATSO NAMLA KHYAB SU CHIO

SANGYE CHOMDEMDE NAMLA KHYAB SU CHIO

DAMPE CHO NAMLA KHYAB SU CHIO

PAKPE GENDUN NAMLA KHYAB SU CHIO

PAWO KANDRO CHOKYONG SUNGMAY TSO
YESHE JI SHEN TANG DENPA NAMLA KHYAB SU CHIO

I take Refuge in the glorious holy Masters
I take Refuge in the deities and yidams gathered in their
mandalas
I take Refuge in the Lords Buddhas
I take Refuge in the Holy Dharmas
I take Refuge in the superior Sangha 僧伽
I take Refuge in the celestial Warriors, the Ladies of
space, Protectors, and Guardians of the Dharma endowed
with the eye of wisdom.[13]

Middle Length Prayer
MA NAMKA TANG NYAMPE SEMCHEN TAMCHE
LAMA SANGYE RINPOCHE LA KHYAB SU CHIO
SANGYE CHO TANG GENDUN NAMLA KHYAB SU CHIO
LAMA YIDAM KHANDRO TSOLA KHYAB SU CHIO
RANG SEM TONGSEL CHO GI KU LA KHYAB SU CHIO

With all beings, my past mothers in number as great as
space
I take Refuge in my Master, the precious Buddha
I take Refuge in the Buddhas, Dharma, and Sangha
I take Refuge in the masters, yidams, Ladies of space
I take Refuge in my own mind, clarity-emptiness, the
Absolute Body.

27

Brief Prayer
LAMA LA KHYAB SU CHIO
SANGYE LA KHYAB SU CHIO
CHO LA KHYAB SU CHIO
GENDUN LA KHYAB SU CHIO

I take Refuge in the Master
I take Refuge in the Buddha
I take Refuge in the Dharma
I take Refuge in the Sangha.

We must recite the Refuge prayer every day. It is the basis for the inner path. Without this Refuge in the Three Jewels, we cannot consider ourselves to be following the Buddha's path. Believing that we can practice the Great Vehicle or the Vajrayana efficiently without taking Refuge would also be a mistake.

This is why, after having taken the vows of Refuge, it is indispensable to commit to reciting one of the Refuge prayers seven times every day. If we do not do it, our vows of Refuge remain a good connection, but they do not permit spiritual development.

During the Refuge ceremony, the lama cuts a strand of hair and knots a protection cord around our neck. A gardener seems to act in the same way, cutting a few flower buds, pruning trees and hanging labels. However, neither plants nor trees have taken Refuge.

If our vows of Refuge are limited to having cut a strand of hair followed by a label, they cannot bring us much. On the contrary, we must nourish them every day through sincere recitation of the prayer that renews and reinforces them; each day, we must think of placing ourselves under the protection of the Three Jewels until Awakening, in order to be spared from suffering, sorrow, danger, and fear, and to be led to Awakening.

8- Chenrezig Practice
It is beneficial to briefly do the short Chenrezig practice every morning using the text in the following section:
a) Taking Refuge and Developing the Mind of Awakening
SANG GYAY CHO DONG TSOK KYI CHOK NAM LA
CHANG CHUB BAR DU DAW NI KYAB SU CHI
DAG GI JIN SOK GYI PAY SO NAM KYI
DRO LA PEN SHIR SANG GYAY DRUB PAR SHO (three times)

Until enlightenment, I take Refuge
In the Buddha, Dharma, and sublime Sangha.
Through the merit engendered by the practice of generosity and other perfections,
May I realize Awakening for the benefit of beings.(three times)

29

Syllable HRI from which Chenrezig appears

Om Ma Ni Pad Me Hung

b) Phase of creation of the deity

DAG SOK KA KYAB SEM CHEN GYI
CHI TSU PAY KAR DA WAY TENG
HRI LAY PA CHO CHEN RAY ZI
KAR SAL O ZER NGA DEN TRO
DZAY DZUM TU JAY CHEN GYI ZIK
CHAK SHI DONG PO TAL JOR DZAY
O NYI SHEL TRENG PAY KAR NAM
DAR DONG RIN CHEN GYEN GYI TRAY
RI DAK PAK PAY TO YOK SOL
O PAK MAY PE U GYEN CHEN
SHAP NYI DOR JAY KYIL TRUNG SHUG
DRI MAY DA WA KYAB TEN PA
KYAB NAY KUN DU NGO WOR GYUR

Above me and all beings of the universe:
A white lotus and moon disc.
On them, the letter HRI from which appears the noble
Chenrezig.
His clear and white body emits five colored rays;
He smiles and looks upon us with compassion.
Of his four hands, the two middle ones are joined,
Of the other two, the right one holds a crystal rosary,
The left, a white lotus.
Silks and jewels adorn him.
A deer skin covers his shoulder,
The Buddha of Infinite Light crowns his head.
He sits in the vajra posture,

To his back is an immaculate moon disc.
He gathers the essence of all Refuges.

Praise:
JO WO KYON GYI MA GU KU DU KAR
DZOK SANG GYAY KYI U LA GYEN
TUK JAY CHEN GYI DRO LA ZIK
CHEN RAY ZI LA CHAK TSAL LO
(three times)

Lord with a white body, stained by no defect,
The perfect Buddha adorns your head.
You look with the eyes of compassion upon all beings.
To you, Chenrezig, I bow down.
(three times)

Then:
DAY TAR TSAY CHIK SOL TAB PAY
PAW PE KU LAY O ZER TRU
MA DAK LAY NANG TRUL SHAY JANG
CHI NU DAY WA CHEN GYI SHING
NANG CHU KYAY DRO LU NGAK SEM
CHEN RAY ZI WANG KU SUNG TUK
NANG DRAK RIK TONG YER MAY GYUR

After praying without distraction,
The body of the noble Chenrezig emits light.
The light dissipates karmically impure appearances and

erroneous understanding.
The outer world becomes the Land of Bliss;
The body, speech, and mind of beings
Become the Body, Speech, and Mind of the Lord Chenrezig.
Appearances, sounds, and cognition are united in emptiness.

Recitation of the mantra
OM MA NI PAD ME HUNG

    We recite one hundred mantras or more. Then, we keep our mind at rest for a while, and we conclude the practice by reciting:

DAG SHEN LU NANG PAK PAY KU
DRA TRAK YI GAY DRUK PE YANG
DREN TOK YE SHAY CHEN PO LONG

My body and others' bodies are the body of Chenrezig,
All sounds are the six syllable melody,
Mental activity is the domain of great wisdom.

GAY WA DI YI NYUR DU DAG
CHEN RAY ZI WANG DRUP GYUR NAY
DRO WA CHIK KYANG MA LU PA
DAY YI SA LA GU PAR SHO

By the virtue of this practice
May I quickly realize the Lord Chenrezig,
Then establish in this state
The totality of beings.

DI TAR GOM DAY GYI PE SO NAM GYI
DAG DANG DAW LA DREL TOK DRO WA KUN
MI TSANG LU DI BOR WA GYUR MA TAK
DAY WA CHEN DU DZU DAY GYAY WAR SHO
KYAY MA TAK TU SA CHU RAB DRU NAY
TRUL PAY CHOK CHUR SHEN DU JAY PAR SHO

By the merit of this meditation and recitation
May I and those related to me,
As soon as we leave this impure body,
Be miraculously born in the Land of Bliss,[14]
Then just after this rebirth, pass through the ten stages
And by emanations, benefit beings in the ten directions.

After this meditation we think:
During the day, whenever I have the opportunity to do
so, while walking, driving, or on the bus, I will
remember to recite the mantra invoking the presence of
Chenrezig, in my mind.

In this way, we take advantage of many moments during the day to recite the mantra, uttering it or if not possible, saying it inwardly. This is the end of the morning practices.

Chenrezig

When we have breakfast, lunch, or dinner, we offer the food that we are about to eat by reciting one or several of the three following offerings:[15]

1- Offering to the Three Jewels

TONPA LAMAY SANGYE RINPOCHE
KHYOBPA LAMAY DAMCHO RINPOCHE
DRENPA LAMAY GENDUN RINPOCHE
KYABNAY KONCHO SUM LA CHOPA BUL

To the precious Buddha, the highest teacher
to the precious Dharma, the highest protection
to the precious Sangha, the highest guide
to you, rare and sublime Refuges, I offer this food.

The Buddha is the highest teacher because he teaches us liberation; the Dharma is the highest protection because it protects us from suffering, first in this world, then in a definitive way through attaining the ultimate; the Sangha is the highest guide because it guides us on the path that leads to exiting the cycle of existences.

2- Offering to the yidam, for instance, Chenrezig

JOWO KYON GI MA GO KUNTO KAR
ZO SANGYE GI U LA GYEN
TUJE CHENGI DROLA ZI
CHENREZIG LA CHO PA BUL

Lord with a white body stained by no defects
the perfect Buddha adorns your head
You look with compassion at all beings
To you Chenrezig, I offer this food.

3- Offering to the root Lama

O MIN CHO KY YING GY POTRANG NAY
DU SUM SANGYE KUN GI NGOWO NY
RANG SEM CHO KU NGON SUM TON ZE PAY
TSAWAY LAMA SHEL TU CHOPA BUL

To you who dwells in the palace of the sublime domain
of the absolute
who are the essence of all the Buddhas of the three times
Who shows me that my mind is Absolute Body
To you Root Lama, I offer this food.

Offering the food that we take accumulates
much merit. It transforms our meals into great
spiritual benefits.

1- Chenrezig Practice
Before going to bed, we sit for a while in front of
our shrine if we have one.
    We can briefly do Chenrezig practice as follows:
    1) Taking Refuge with the prayer SANGYE CHO
    TANG...
    2) Reciting 100 or more mantras
    3) Silent meditation (shinay) for a while
    4) Dedicating from DA SHEN LU NANG PAKPAY
    KU until DAY YI SA LA GO PAR SHO

2- Assessment of the Day
After the Chenrezig practice, we look at the past
day in order to assess it.
    If we have committed negative deeds, we regret
them and disavow them, and we wish, "Tomorrow,
may I not make the same mistakes."
    If we have accomplished positive deeds, we
think of dedicating their merit to all beings so they
can attain Awakening.

3- Prayer to Be Reborn into the Land of Bliss
Next, we recite the brief prayer to be reborn into
the Land of Bliss.

EMAHO!

NGO TSAR SANGYE NANGWA TAYE TANG

YE SU JOWO TUJE CHENPO TANG

YONTU SEMPA TU CHEN TOB NAMLA

SANGYE JANGSEM PAKME KHOR GI KOR

DEKI NGOTSAR PAKTU MEPA YI

DEWACHEN SHE JAWO SHINGKHAM DER

DANI DINE TSEPO GYUR MATAK

KYEWA SHEN GI BAR MA CHO PA RU

DERU KYE NE NANGTOL SHEL TONG SHO

DEKE DAGI MONLAM TABPA DI

CHO CHU SANGYE GE JANG SEM TAMCHE KI

GEL ME DRUBPAR JINGILAB TU SOL

TEYATA PENTSANDRIYA AWA BODHANI SOHA

Emaho!

Wonderful Buddha of Infinite Light

on your right there is the Lord of Great Compassion[16]

on your left, there is the Bodhisattva with Great Powers[17]

*and you are surrounded by numberless Buddhas and
Bodhisattvas.*

This world called Land of Bliss

is happiness and well-being, wonderful, and endless.

As soon as I leave this life

without taking any other births in the meantime

may I be reborn into it and see the face of Infinite Light.

Buddhas and Bodhisattvas of the ten directions

please grant your blessing in order that the wishes uttered like this be realized without obstacle.

TEYATA PENTSANDRIYA AWA BODHANI SOHA

4- Emptying the Offering Bowls

We empty the water offerings made in the morning. We dry the bowls and place them upside down.

As in the morning, we prostrate three times in front of the shrine reciting the prostration mantra.

5- At the Time of Going to Sleep

a) Posture

We go to sleep in the lion posture. Lying down on the right side, with the right hand on the cheek, with stretched legs, and the left hand on the left thigh. It is the posture of the Buddha when he was dying. The benefits of this posture are said to be great.

b) Visualization

— We imagine that the Buddha, lama, or yidam is above our head. We think, "Tomorrow, at such and such a time, I will get up and do my practice," and we fall asleep in a spirit of devotion.

— We can also imagine that the luminous lama (the Buddha or a yidam), the size of a thumb, is in our heart[18] in an abode of light. We fall asleep with this thought.

41

Manjushri

Using Circumstances Mindfully

1- Happiness
During the day, we encounter many joys. If we do not use them as a support for spiritual practice, they are useless. However, if we know how to integrate them into practice, they allow us to create new positive karma. Otherwise, we exhaust our potential for happiness without accumulating any new positive karma. If we use the beneficial potential without recharging it, it becomes exhausted. It is like eating a piece of fruit. Once eaten, nothing is left. To transform our joys and happiness into spiritual practice, we must think that we do not keep them for ourselves but dedicate them to the happiness of others. It is like sowing the seed of the piece of fruit we have eaten. Because of the seed, other good fruit will ripen in the future. By dedicating it, our potential for happiness does not exhaust itself. Present happiness prepares the way for future happiness.

When we are happy, we dedicate our joy to the assembly of happiness:

May happiness fill all of the space![19]

When we feel good, physically or mentally, these circumstances give us joy or happiness. When we are successful in whatever we undertake, we must become aware of this and wish that all beings know the same happiness.

If we want to, we can also support this thought by the visualization of *taking and sending*—in this case, we imagine that we exhale white light spreading to all beings and bestowing happiness upon them.

On the other hand, our happiness and joy should not be an occasion for vain satisfaction or attachment. We must remind ourselves that happiness and joy are the fruits of past positive karma; therefore, they are passing and changing, lacking any definitive characteristic.

2- *Suffering*

When we suffer, if we do not use this suffering as a support of spiritual practice, the situation is even more difficult to bear because it is complicated by rejection, worry, or anxiety, even though these cannot help us to escape from suffering.

There are two benefits in integrating suffering with practice:

— Suffering and worry become less important and therefore decrease.

— Thinking that we take upon ourselves the suffering of all beings, we engender much positive karma.

When we suffer, we take the suffering upon ourselves:

May I drain the ocean of suffering of the world.

We reflect as follows:

My sufferings are the results of negative deeds that I have accomplished in the past. They are, therefore, impermanent and will end when negative karma is exhausted.

I am not the only one to suffer, all beings encounter suffering, pain, difficulty, and failure. Many of them suffer even more than I do.

In fact, it is useless for others to suffer. My suffering is enough. May I take all sufferings within my suffering.

We can also use the visualization of *taking and sending*, thinking that we inhale a black light through which we take upon us the suffering of others.

If we felt no joy or suffering, we could disregard these instructions. However, this never happens.

3- Illness

When we are ill, we reflect as follows.

"Pains I now feel are the results of negative deeds done in the past. I, myself, am responsible for them.

Other beings who have accumulated more negative karma suffer even more than I do. May illness and suffering of all beings melt into mine; may all beings be free from suffering and illness."

Thinking like this, we do the visualization of *taking and sending*. We imagine that we inhale black breath through which we take the illness of all beings upon ourselves, then we exhale a white breath that gives happiness and health to all beings.

Sometimes, we become aware that the experience of this illness is possible only because of false perception engendered by the absence of realization of the mode of being of the mind. From the point of view of ultimate realty, what is called illness does not exist. Being ill is a little like dreaming that we are ill. We would feel the suffering of a illness that exists nowhere but in our dream. Our illness has in fact no reality in and of itself.

We can also imagine that our lama, seen as the union of the Three Jewels, is present in the ill part of our body, and that in his or her luminous body

Sangye Menla

药师佛

flows a nectar that spreads into the ill area and relieves us.

Finally, if we know the practice, we can pray to Sangye Menla (Medicine Buddha) and recite his mantra.

4- Small occasions

We can use many gestures of daily life in many circumstances to sow in our mind thoughts oriented toward Awakening. To do so, we can retain and use the wishes taught by the Buddha himself in the *Sutra of Great Approximation.*

— When we dress:
May I dress with the cloth of scruple and modesty.

— When we put on a belt:
May I be tied up with the belt of sacred vows and commitments.

— When we open a door:
May the door of profound reality open.

— When we close a door:
May the doors of inferior realms be closed.

— When we walk:
May I progress on the path of Awakening.

— When we ride (drive, take a train, and so on):
May I ride the horse of diligence.

— When we cross a river (on a bridge, a boat):
May I cross the ocean of samsara.

— When we go up a hill or stairs:
May I climb the path of liberation.

— When we arrive at our destination:
May I arrive at the city of nirvana.

— When we encounter a master or an excellent person:
May I encounter and follow a perfect master.

— When we see a representation of the Three Jewels:
May I be reborn into the Buddhas' Pure Land.

5- When We Eat Meat
Eating meat from a killed animal is a negative deed. It is better not to eat any meat at all.

If, however, because of circumstances, we cannot abstain from eating meat, at least we must avoid causing an animal to be killed for our consumption. We must not order a live animal to be killed for ourselves.

Meat bought at the butcher comes from animals killed for general consumption and not directly from an order we have given. Eating this meat is also a negative deed but it is less serious.

When we eat meat, we must direct our compassion toward the animal that was killed, recite the Names of the Buddhas, Chenrezig mantra, or other mantras, and blow on the meat. We wish at the same time that the animal be delivered from inferior realms and be born into the Land of Bliss.

Doing this not only brings help to the animal but also diminishes the strength of negative karma accumulated through eating meat.

6- Television

Since television did not exist at the time of the Buddha, he did not talk about it. However, nowadays in the West, most people spend time in front of the television.

Watching television occasionally is not harmful, but devoting many hours is harmful from several points of view.

— Firstly, it wastes much time. Two hours spent watching television is two hours that we might have spent practicing the Dharma and, therefore, accumulating great positive potential. Or with these two hours, we could have done something useful. Or with these two hours, we might have rested. It is better to sleep and be peaceful than to waste time in front of the television.

— Secondly, television is harmful to our mind. We are usually inhabited by many thoughts. Nourishing our mind with all kinds of news and fantasy will only increase the flow of thoughts and will give us neither peace nor happiness.

For those of us who practice the Dharma, it is best not to watch television or at least to give it very little time.

When, however, it happens that we watch television, let us do it with moderation and try to use it as a support of practice by applying the following methods.

Offering: When we see beautiful landscapes, flowers, mountains, the ocean, or all kinds of beautiful things on television, we think of them as offerings to the Three Jewels and to our spiritual master.

Compassion: When we see a drama that depicts suffering, war, illness, quarrels, or death, let us think, "Beings suffer in many ways. May all beings be free from suffering and obtain Awakening."

51

Impermanence: Television shows us changes that occur in the world, situations that successively improve or deteriorate. We think that all phenomena of samsara are transitory and changing. Good or bad, everything changes.

In fact, the true show is the world itself. Television only offers us a reduced sample, a small imitation. It is necessary to know how to apply the few examples that television gives us to the entire world, reflecting upon them to understand their universality.

Absence of reality of appearances: What appears on the screen of the television presents some levels of reality. We see various things, people acting, talking, reflecting. In fact, it is only a mock up of reality. Outside of the screen appearances there are no human beings, no actions, no words, no thoughts. All phenomena have this same nature, they are simple appearances devoid of a reality on their own, similar to a dream.

Looking at our mind: We become aware in moments that television is an object known by the subject that is our mind. We then turn our mind to itself and let it relax and rest in peace.

By occasionally watching television and using these methods, television cannot harm us. But only under these conditions.

7- A Cure for Each Emotion

Each day, the five poisons, that is, the five conflicting emotions, arise in our mind several times with more or less intensity. There are various methods of facing these phenomena. Among them, arise the following reflections.

a) Desire and Attachment

The terms *desire* and *attachment* do not only apply to the relationship between human beings but also to attraction exerted on us by wealth, food, clothes, material goods, pleasant sounds, perfumes, and so on. Except for attraction between human beings, we usually do not pay much attention to other kinds of desire. However, all moves that carry us toward sense objects—forms, sounds, smells, taste, and objects of touch—are also desire.

When desire arises within ourselves, we must first recognize it, and then we must understand that even if the desired object can bring some pleasure, the pleasure will transform one day into suffering. The Buddha said that giving ourselves to pleasure is like licking honey on a razor blade: a pleasant sensation soon followed by pain.

This does not mean that we can never benefit from any of the pleasure of this world. But the stronger the attachment, the stronger the suffering. If we lick honey greedily on a razor blade, we will deeply cut our tongue; if we lick it carefully knowing that the sharp blade is hidden under the honey, our tongue will be lightly cut. Also, we must know how to benefit from worldly pleasures with caution and moderation. Generally, we do not know how to be moderate because we are not aware of the razor blade hidden beneath the honey. Attracted by the honey, we lick it without moderation and deeply hurt ourselves.

b) Aversion and Anger

When we are under the influence of aversion or anger, let us think like this: "I remember that all beings have been my mothers and fathers, and I develop patience and compassion.

When someone gets angry at me, I suffer.

When I get angry at someone, the latter feels similar suffering. On the contrary, when someone is kind to me, I am happy. To make others happy, I must therefore show the same kindness as the kindness I expect from others."

c) Blindness 無明

Blindness is not to know what is beneficial or negative from a spiritual point of view. The remedy is to study the Dharma, to understand the law of karma, the nature of the mind, and so on.

d) Pride 我慢

To appear in our mind, pride is supported by many pretexts such as beauty, power, wealth, culture, intelligence, or some capabilities in one domain or another. Pride results from a lack of reflection. However, if we reflect, it is easy to see that there are people more beautiful, powerful, wealthy, educated, intelligent, or more capable. We then see that believing that we are superior is no more than a sign of stupidity.

Once upon a time, there was a frog living in a well. He looked at his dwelling as an immense surface of water that had no equal anywhere. Another frog who lived at the seaside passed by one day and jumped on the rim of the well to see what was at the bottom.

"Where do you come from?" asked the frog on the bottom.

"I come from the seaside."

"Sea? How large is the sea?"

"Oh, it is really very large."

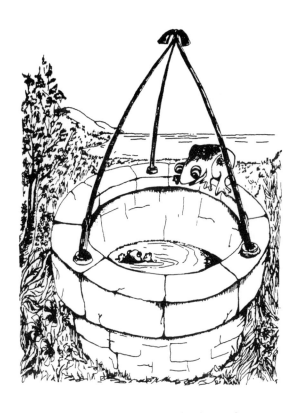

Sea? How large is the sea?

"As large as one fourth of my well?" asked the proud frog that could not really see what the other frog meant by "very large."

"No, much larger."

"As large as half of my well?" asked the well dweller with some disbelief.

"No, even larger."

"As large as my well then?"

"No, larger than your well."

The frog thought that the visitor was teasing him. A surface of water larger than his well? What stupidity! However, to be sure, he asked if he could see the sea.

The other frog agreed and both of them went hopping to the seaside. Poor well-frog! Such immensity! It was too much for his mind, and he collapsed. Such was his pride that he could not bear the thought of anything larger than his well.

Pride makes us suffer and makes us create suffering for others. If we actually have certain qualities, pride will add nothing. If we have no such qualities, pride will not give them to us.

e) Jealousy

When we are jealous of another person, when we resent the thought of another possessing what we do not have or that happier events take place for this person, we must see that our unhappiness makes no sense.

On the contrary, we must put ourselves in the place of the other person.

"If I am in the position of someone receiving something good, would someone else's jealousy make sense? No. Likewise, my own envy is only stupidity.

"What good happens to others is not something taken away from me. Even if I could deprive others of what they have, this would give me nothing.

"Jealousy is only a thought expressing the confusion of my mind."

Briefly, we can consider that there is an antidote for each poison.

— desire: recognizing that pleasure and suffering have the same nature.
— aversion: love and compassion
— blindness: knowledge
— pride: considering others to be superior
— jealousy: rejoicing at happiness enjoyed by others

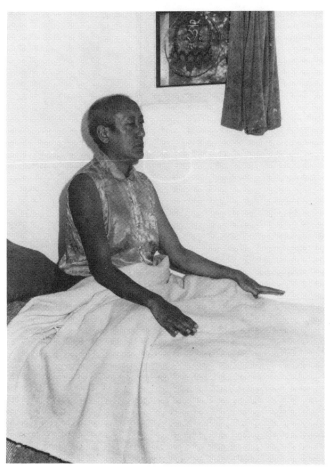

Breathing exercises

Washing oneself, one thinks that one is purified.

Prostrating in front of the shrine

Meditating in front of the shrine

"May the ocean of suffering of the world be dried up." Bokar Rinpoche recovering from surgery.

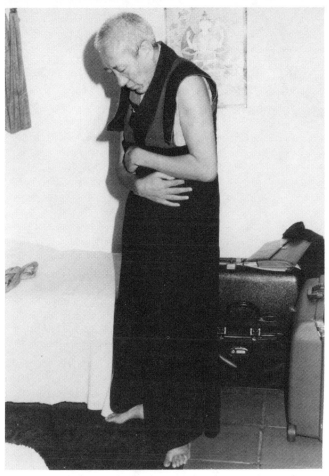

"May I dress with the cloth of scruple and modesty."

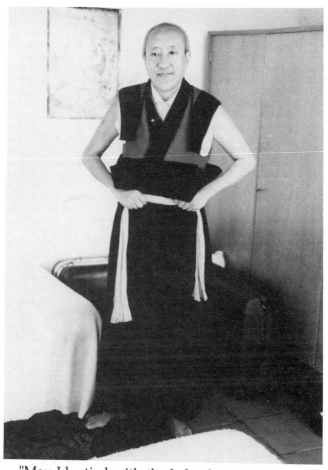

"May I be tied with the belt of commitments."

"May I climb the path of liberation."

"May I open the door of profound reality."

"May I close the door of inferior realms."

"May I go forward on the path of Awakening."

"May I ride the horse of diligence."

"May I arrive at the city of nirvana."

"May I meet with a perfect Master and follow his or her instructions." (Bokar Rinpoche welcoming Kalu Rinpoche)

Right Conduct

All phenomena, including our mind, are included in the two truths, relative truth and ultimate truth. As for those of us who have not realized the mode of being of the mind, we do not really understand these two truths and what they are.

To realize this mode of being, we must practice within the framework of relative truth, in particular to harmonize our conduct with the understanding that happiness proceeds from positive deeds and suffering from negative ones.

Positive and negative deeds exist in relative truth. From the point of view of the ultimate, they lack an existence of their own. However, we have not yet realized this ultimate truth, and as long as we have not attained it, the link between deeds and their karmic consequences remains unbreakable.

We must know, unmistakenly, what must be adopted and what is to be rejected. In this way, we avoid suffering and know happiness in the context of relative truth. Positive conduct of the body, speech, and mind necessarily produces happiness; negative conduct of body, speech, and mind necessarily leads to suffering.

Generally, we call positive deeds any activity of our body, speech, and mind that contributes to another person's benefit, immediately or later, through its effects.

On the other hand, we call negative deeds any activity of our body, speech, and mind that causes another person's suffering, immediately or later, through its effects.

The details of this ethic are complex, but the directions are simple, presented in the form of a classification of ten positive deeds and ten negative deeds.[20]

TEN POSITIVE DEEDS
Three Positive Deeds of the Body
1) Protecting life, for instance buying live fish, shellfish, or crustaceans at the market and releasing them into the ocean.

2) Practicing generosity, if only giving a hungry person or a dog or even a fish some food.

3) Being faithful to one's spouse or companion. Being faithful in this life brings inner peace. Unfaithfulness, on the contrary, leads to complications and suffering.

Four Positive Deeds of Speech
1) Speaking the truth, talking frankly.

2) Through our speech, bringing people together who are separated by misunderstanding.

3) Talking softly, kindly, and in a pleasant way to others.

4) Using speech in a useful way, especially by reciting mantras and prayers.

Three Positive Deeds of the Mind
1) Contentment: Being satisfied by our situation and with what we have. Thinking, "It is well, it is enough for me. It is well like this." Contentment is the root of happiness. Without contentment, we necessarily meet with suffering.

2) Kindness: Sincere wish for the happiness of others.

3) Right conceptions: Developing understanding of the Dharma, the law of karma, the qualities of Awakening, and the nature of the mind. Even if our knowledge is now insufficient to establish certitude, we must think: "All this might be true. I do not understand everything now, but it is the limits of

my own mind that cause this. I wish, in the future to obtain a clear, thorough understanding."

THE TEN NEGATIVE DEEDS
Three Negative Deeds of the Body
1) Intentionally killing, not just a human being but even an animal, even an insect. Most people are not aware that other human beings share the faculty to feel happiness and suffering. Or when they are aware of this, they do not understand that animals, even insects have the same power to feel, hope, and fear. Being sensitive to happiness and suffering is, however, the common denominator of all living beings: humans, cows, goats, sheep, flies, or the smallest insect. Killing them is a negative deed.

2) Voluntarily take and take without permission that which does not belong to us.

3) Not being faithful to one's spouse or companion.

Four Negative Deeds of Speech
1) Fooling someone by telling lies for one's own interest.

2) Talking in a way that creates dissension.

3) Saying hurtful words.

4) Engaging in useless conversation, words without spiritual benefit, and those useless even for ordinary activity. This idle talk makes us lose time, and arouses desire, anger, jealousy, and often ends up creating dissension among those with whom we converse.

Three Negative Deeds of the Mind
1) Envy: On the one hand, wishing to possess what belongs to others; on the other hand, being very attached to our own possessions.

2) Ill will: Having our mind turned against benefiting others.

3) False conception: Thinking that the law of karma is not true, not believing in the qualities of Awakening, or in the shortcomings of conditioned existence. It is not to ignore these various things that constitutes an erroneous conception *per se*, but rather it is to reject the validity of these things when we know them. From the point of view of the Buddha's teachings, the joys and sufferings of the world do not just occur by chance. They are neither the creation of a superior god nor the results of our ability or inability to manage our life. In fact, happiness and suffering arise from our karma; that is, they are the results of the activity of our body,

speech, and mind. First, we produce a thought, then, we put it to work physically or verbally. We create karma by doing this. Karma necessarily accumulates through one or several of the three doors, the body door, the speech door, and the mind door. This is why the classification of deeds follows this division between body, speech, and mind.

A Few Mantras

Chenrezig Mantra, to develop love and compassion
OM MA NI PAD ME HUNG

Tara Mantra, against fear and danger 度母咒
(心咒)
(根本咒)
OM TARE TUTTARE TURE SOHA

Dorje Sempa Mantra, for purifying
OM BENZA SATO HUNG 短咒
(除障)

Ambitious Mantra for long life
OM AMARANIZI WENTIYE SOHA

Sangye Menla Mantra, against illness 药师佛
TEYATA OM BEKAZE BEKAZE MAHA BAKAZE RAZA
SAMOGATE SOHA

Manjushri Mantra to develop ordinary and spiritual
knowledge
OM ARA PATSANA DHI DHI DHI 文殊

79

In the following pages, you can add other deities'
mantras whose empowerment you have received.

Additional Mantras

Amitayus

Endnotes

1. Sutras are the texts collecting the teachings given by the Buddha in the framework of the Small and Great Vehicles; tantras gather teachings of the Vajrayana, the Diamond Vehicle.

2. The mode of being of the mind is the true nature of the mind, beyond illusions created by subject-object duality.

3. Relative truth is concerned with the mode of manifestation of phenomena; ultimate truth is concerned with the nonmanifested aspect of reality.

4. The word *deed* must be understood in a larger sense than usual. It applies not only to physical actions but also to speech and mind activity. In this sense, a thought is a deed; an utterance is a deed. A deed is not understood here as being necessarily directed to an object. Praying, reciting mantras, meditating are positive deeds, just as generosity or protecting life.

5. Dedicating the merit of a positive deed means that we wish that the positive potential it has necessarily engendered will benefit all beings.

6. We may think that more than 15 minutes are necessary to accomplish the following exercises. In fact, once the habit is formed, 15 minutes are sufficient.

7. Samsara: cycle of conditioned existence, that is, the world where beings are born unceasingly, in more or less painful conditions. Getting out of samsara is attaining liberation.

8. These few lines do not have to be recited as they are. They point to the way in which we must give a positive momentum to our mind for the day that is starting.

9. The seven offerings are eight in reality because the two first ones are counted as one.

10. The Three Jewels are the Buddha, Dharma (his teachings), and Sangha (community of those who have attained high levels of realization and transmit the Dharma). The Three Roots are lamas, yidams, and protectors. (See note 13)

11. The Thus-Gone means the one who is gone in thatness, the essence of phenomena as it is and who is no longer fooled by appearances; the Victor over the enemies refers to the victory over inner enemies.

12. There are many other forms of Refuge that may be used.

13. The yidams are manifestations of Awakening in the field of light with whom a link is established through empowerments, meditation, and recitation of mantras. Chenrezig, for instance, is a yidam. There are many

others. Dharma means spiritual teachings. Superior Sangha represents the community of realized beings. Other members of the spiritual community form the ordinary sangha. The celestial Warriors (Dakas), Ladies of the space (Dakinis), protectors, and guardians of the Dharma are beings living on higher levels than us, acting as messengers and protectors. They appear to correspond to the different types of angels in Christian theology.

14. The Land of Bliss is the domain of pure manifestation of Amitabha Buddha (Buddha of Infinite Light).

15. There are many other food offering prayers.

16. Chenrezig.

17. Vajrapani. 大勢至菩薩 (金剛悸)

18. We do not refer to the physical organ here but to the heart chakra considered as the seat of the mind in the body. It is in the axis of the body, at the level of the physical heart.

19. This quotation and the quotation in the paragraph on suffering are the words of the Buddha himself consigned in the *Sutra of Great Approximation.*

20. It is necessary to understand the base of this ethic. It does not correspond to an arbitrary decision imposing a moral code whose justification is obscure. It does not

refer to recompense or punishment given from above. It simply derives from the description of invisible reality done by the Buddha who had a direct vision of the inherent consequences of any deed. It is a little like the driving rules of happiness: "red flare: hazard," "red light," "green light," or *freeway to freedom*.

Glossary

ACCUMULATION OF MERIT: Practice of positive deeds allowing us to store energy for the progression on the spiritual path. This accumulation of merit can be done through the practice of giving, making offerings, reciting mantras, visualizing deities, and so on.

AWAKENING: State of Buddhahood.

BEINGS: There are six classes of beings: gods, demigods, human beings, animals, hungry ghosts, and hell beings.

BODHICITTA: Aspiration to obtain Awakening in order to help all beings.

BODHISATTVA: Being who follows the bodhicitta path and seeks to obtain Awakening not only for oneself but for the sake of all beings. An ordinary being who commits to practice bodhicitta. One who has attained Awakening and dwells in one of the ten stages of the bodhisattvas. A bodhisattva can be physically present in our world or abide in domains of more subtle manifestation.

BODY: Ordinary physical body. State of possessing numerous qualities, in Sanskrit, *kaya*.

BUDDHA NATURE: Potential of Awakening inherent in all beings.

BUDDHA: One who has awakened. A person, as the historical Buddha Sakyamuni. In Tibetan, *Sangyay*. *Sang* means purified from the conflicting emotions, duality and ignorance; *gyay* means that the infinite potential of qualities of a being is awakened.

BUDDHAHOOD: Awakened state characterized by wisdom (as knowledge of the true nature of phenomena and their manifestation in the three times), compassion for every being, and power to help all beings.

CHENREZIG (Tibetan): Avalokitesvara (Sanskrit). Buddha of Compassion. Most popular Tibetan deity, his mantra is OM MA NI PAD ME HUNG. See *Chenrezig, Lord of Love* (ClearPoint Press).

COMPASSION: Aspiration to liberate all beings from suffering and cause of suffering.

CONFLICTING EMOTIONS: Desire-attachment, hatred-aversion, ignorance or mental dullness, jealousy, pride, and so on.

DEDICATION: Aspiration that any merit accumulated through our positive deeds serves to attain Awakening for the benefit of all beings.

DHARMA: Buddha's teachings or the spiritual path.

DHARMAKAYA: Absolute Body, designating a state beyond any spacial or temporal determination; corresponds to emptiness.

DORJE SEMPA (Tibetan): Vajrasattva (Sanskrit), deity of the Vajrayana who is the source of purification practices. The practice of Dorje Sempa includes a visualization as well as recitation of a mantra.

FIVE POISONS: Desire, anger, ignorance, pride, and jealousy.

KARMA: The law of karma describes the process of cause and effect. It is a three-phase process:
— a deed leaves an imprint in the mind of the one who acts (cause).
— this deed is stored in the potential of consciousness and is slowly ripening.
— this process is actualized in a particular form of suffering or joy (result).

LAMA (Tibetan): Guru (Sanskrit). A spiritual teacher.

LOVE: Aspiration to bring happiness to all beings.

MANTRA: Sacred sounds, the repetition of which helps the mind purify itself and develop its potential for

Awakening. For example, the mantra of Chenrezig is OM MA NI PAD ME HUNG.

MEDITATION POSTURE: *Bodhisattva posture:* Seated with legs crossed, left heel against the perineum, right foot and leg are bent flat in front. *Vairocana posture:* It is also called seven-point posture: 1. legs in vajra position, 2. hands in meditation mudra, 3. straight spine, 4. open shoulders, 5. chin down, 6. eyes gazing in space downward and 7. relaxed tongue. *Vajra posture:* It is also called "diamond posture". Seated with legs crossed, first, the left foot on the right thigh and the right foot on the left thigh.

MIND: This term can refer to the ordinary functioning of the mind called "psyche" as well as the absolute, non-dual pure essence of the mind beyond the fluctuations that may affect the ordinary mind.

NIRVANA: Literally "extinguished," cessation. Early definition included liberation from conditioned existence, ignorance, and conflicting emotions. Later definition was expanded to include the development of great compassion through skillful means.

OBSTACLES: Circumstances not favorable to the dharma practice which can be experienced as external obstacles, internal obstacles (sickness), and secret obstacles (our own thoughts).

PURIFICATION: All negative deeds done in this life and in the past lives have left imprints in our potential of consciousness. These imprints will ripen, engendering suffering and obstacles to our spiritual practice. Purification will neutralize these imprints in order to avoid or reduce their effects. A qualified teacher might designate specific practice to do in order to purify oneself.

ROOT LAMA: Generally, the lama we recognize as "our" teacher, who gives us initiations, instructions to practice, and explanation of the texts. More particularly, the lama who allows us to directly experience the true nature of the mind.

SAKYAMUNI: Literally "wise man of the Sakya," name of the historical Buddha who lived in the 6th century B.C.E.

SAMSARA: Cycle of conditioned existence in which each being is born and dies. It is characterized by suffering, ignorance, impermanence, and illusion.

SANGHA: Community of Buddhist practitioners. One distinguishes ordinary sangha from the Noble Sangha which is composed of those who have attained the bodhisattva levels.

SHINAY (Tibetan): Shamatha (Sanskrit). Mental calming. Meditation practice which frees the mind from reacting to the play of thoughts. It can be done with or without support.

SUFFERING: Generally it is analyzed on three levels:
— suffering of suffering: physical and mental pain experienced by all beings.
— suffering of change: one experiences suffering when happiness ends.
— suffering of conditioned existence is suffering one undergoes because of the deluded nature of samsara. It ends only when one attains Awakening.

SUFFERING OF THE HUMAN REALM: Birth, aging, sickness, death, sorrow, grief, despair, getting things we do not like, losing things we like, not getting what we wish for, and so on.

TAKING REFUGE: Placing oneself under the protection of the Buddha, Dharma, and Sangha (the Three Jewels). In the Vajrayana, one also takes Refuge in the Three Roots, lamas, yidams, and dharma protectors.

VAJRAYANA: Path of Buddhism also called "Diamond Vehicle" referring to the part of the Buddha's teachings written in texts of an esoteric nature called tantras. It uses recitation of mantras, visualizations of deities, and works with the subtle winds or energies.

VEILS: That which obscures our Buddha nature such as ignorance, latent conditioning, dualistic perception, conflicting emotion, karmic veils, and so on.

VISUALIZATION: Creation of a mental image used as a support in a meditation or ritual. These images can be geometrical forms or deities, moving or still. This exercise is not dependent upon visual perception but upon inner faculty of imagining.

YIDAM: A personal deity expressing the pure nature of the mind. A deity upon which one meditates after having received an initiation.

Index

Other Books Published by ClearPoint Press

By Kalu Rinpoche
- *Excellent Buddhism*
- *Profound Buddhism*
- *Secret Buddhism*

By Bokar Rinpoche
- *Chenrezig Lord of Love*
- *Meditation Advice to Beginners*
- *Death and the Art of Dying in Tibetan Buddhism*
- *Profound Wisdom of the Heart Sutra*
- *Opening the Door to Certainty*
- *Taking the Bodhisattva Vow*